Legends of Hollywood: The Life and Legacy of Greta Garbo

By Charles River Editors

Greta Garbo in 1935

About Charles River Editors

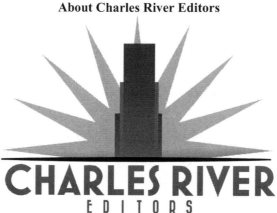

Charles River Editors was founded by Harvard and MIT alumni to provide superior editing and original writing services, with the expertise to create digital content for publishers across a vast range of subject matter. In addition to providing original digital content for third party publishers, Charles River Editors republishes civilization's greatest literary works, bringing them to a new generation via ebooks.

Introduction

Greta Garbo in 1939

Greta Garbo (1905-1990)

"Her instinct, her mastery over the machine, was pure witchcraft. I cannot analyze this woman's acting. I only know that no one else so effectively worked in front of a camera." – Bette Davis

Of all the great movie stars, there may be none more enigmatic than Greta Garbo, who remains internationally famous despite the fact her life and career raise more questions than answers. How did a Swedish actress with very little film acting experience in her native land arrive in the United States and achieve instant stardom? Most actresses had to wait years before they were offered starring roles in major films, yet Garbo was ushered to the front of the line and perched atop the MGM pantheon at a time in which it was the studio par excellence. How was she able to transition from silent films to "talkies" so fluidly, giving many of her most decorated performances during the 1930s? While stars like Charlie Chaplin never recovered from cinema's transition to synchronized sound, Garbo flourished, which is made all the more amazing by the fact she had a foreign accent that could easily have alienated American audiences and threatened her career. Finally, and perhaps most mystifyingly of all, why would Garbo retire in 1941, at just 36 years of age and two years removed from *Ninotchka*, arguably her most acclaimed film?

As unique as Greta Garbo and her career were, there is no denying the impact that she had on audiences, both critics and working-class viewers. Not only was she the most lucrative star in the country by 1928, she also provoked awe from some of the most venerable film and cultural theorists, who attempted to articulate exactly what it was about her that proved so arresting (Swenson). Writing about her in a famous essay devoted to her face, Roland Barthes asserted, "Garbo still belongs to that moment in cinema when capturing the human face still plunged audiences into the deepest ecstasy, when one literally lose oneself in a human image as one would in a philtre, when the face represented a kind of absolute state of the flesh, which could be neither reached nor renounced. A few years earlier the face of Valentino was causing suicides; that of Garbo still partakes of the same rule of Courtly Love, where the flesh gives rise to mystical feelings of perdition." Barthes' description hints at how Garbo's face was the primary attraction of her films, to the point that she achieved a spellbinding influence that made her one of the true goddesses of film history.

At the same time, for as famous as Greta Garbo is as an actress, her films are not remembered so positively, if they are remembered at all. While Garbo herself was nominated on three occasions for the Academy Award for Best Actress, only one film of hers, *Grand Hotel* (1932), was even nominated for an Academy Award for Best Picture. For the most part, Garbo acted in films that were seemingly well beneath her, which was certainly the case with her films from the silent era. During the late 1920s, for example, she was routinely paired with leading man John Gilbert, yet out of the films they appeared in together — *Flesh and the Devil* (1926), *Love* (1927), *A Woman of Affairs* (1928), and *Queen Christina* (1933) — only the latter is well-remembered today. Even the first film for which she was nominated for an Oscar, *Romance* (1930), is commemorated only by Garbo's most fervent admirers. Ironically enough, it was just as Garbo neared the end of her career that she was just beginning to star in more critically revered films, movies such as *Anna Karenina* (1935), *Camille* (1936), and most of all, *Ninotchka* (1939). For the most part, the career of Greta Garbo comprises a paradoxical mix of exquisite performances lodged inside mediocre pictures, creating an inseparable gulf between the indelible impression left by her acting and the utterly forgettable movies in which she appeared.

Legends of Hollywood: The Life and Legacy of Greta Garbo explores the life and career of Greta Garbo, analyzing her fame and how a notably shy young girl rose to the top of Hollywood. Along with pictures of important people, places, and events, you will learn about Garbo like never before, in no time at all.

Chapter 1: A Long Way from Fame

Like many actresses of the era, Greta Garbo changed her name when entering show business; her name at birth was Greta Louisa Gustafsson, and she was born on September 18, 1905, in Sodermalm, a working-class division of Stockholm. Greta was the youngest of three children born to Anna Lovisa and Karl Alfred Gustafsson, and at the time of her birth, her parents were relatively advanced in age, at least for the time period. Karl was 34 years old, while Anna was a year younger. Greta's older brother, Sven, was a full seven years older than her, and her sister, Maria, had been born in 1903. Neither Karl nor Anna had been born in Stockholm, although Stockholm was where they first met. Karl originally hailed from Frinnaryd. and Anna was raised in Hogsby.

It would be impossible to understand Greta's life or childhood without placing it in its proper historical context. Sweden industrialized quite late, so Karl and Anna were raised in rural, impoverished farming settings. Karl had spent the first 20 years of his life working on his family's farm, and as a result, he led a sheltered existence, even though he was tall for the time period (standing roughly 6') and was considered quite attractive. Greta would inherit his delicate features (Payne). Meanwhile, Anna was the daughter of a peasant from Hogsby, an extremely small village in the southeastern corner of the country. After meeting in Stockholm, Anna became pregnant despite the fact that they had still yet to get married. Fully aware that raising children prior to getting married was forbidden in their families, Karl and Anna eloped to the city, which was still in the process of undergoing industrialization. For Greta's parents, Stockholm represented a setting in which they could have a fresh economic start, although this should not be interpreted to suggest that they were any less religious than their families had been. Indeed, Karl and Anna were God-fearing and maintained a strong fidelity toward their familial heritage (Payne). They maintained meticulous records of their family history and placed great emphasis on maintaining a tight-knight family. Accordingly, Greta was exceptionally close to her parents and siblings throughout her upbringing.

Even though her family loved her a great deal, Greta Garbo could not have been born into a more inauspicious environment. Her father toiled from job to job, variously employed as a street cleaner, grocer, factory worker, and even butcher's assistant, and after Greta was born, Anna accepted employment in a jam factory. Regardless of which job her parents happened to occupy at any given point of time, the Gustafsson clan barely possessed enough means to survive, and they lived in a three-bedroom flat in Blekingegatan, regarded as a slum. While it is notoriously difficult to clearly ascertain Garbo's attitudes toward her personal life, Greta does appear to have been negatively disposed toward, if not disturbed, by her family situation as a child, because she forever refused to divulge what her father did for employment. After becoming rich as an adult, Garbo would prove exceptionally careful and savvy in managing her money, perhaps a consequence of never having sufficient means as a child.

Despite struggling to make ends meet, Greta's childhood was relatively standard in many ways. As was the custom in her village, she matriculated in local schools just before her 7th birthday, but the experience was not particularly positive. Throughout her childhood, Garbo never embraced school, and her report cards reflected that; she scored highly in citizenship and was well-behaved, but her coursework was mediocre at best (Payne). As she grew older, her marks improved, but she was never regarded as one of the stronger students in her class (Paris).

However, even as a young child, Greta was quite precocious as an actress; she and local children staged theatrical productions, and despite her innate shyness, she enjoyed performing (Paris). Greta also daydreamed regularly, which no doubt offered a temporary escape from conditions that were often adverse, but was also indicative of an early manifestation of the deep interiority that would define Greta as an adult. Indeed, during her entire life, Greta maintained an appreciation for solitude and enjoyed being left alone with her thoughts.

Young Greta

As Greta's acting pursuits make clear, there was room for leisure in her life, even if it was continuously counterbalanced by extreme adversity. When she was 9, rationing was implemented in Sweden, and she was constantly underfed during her youth (Payne). Making matters worse, the family's troubles were exacerbated by the fact that her father drank heavily, even though that did not take him away from his family. At the same time, no matter how difficult conditions became, Greta was blessed with a beautiful figure, and when she reached her teenage years, she began to grow into the woman she would become (Payne). As a child, she had been extremely thin (no doubt due in part to the fact there was not sufficient food in the household), but her physical development eventually brought about a more voluptuous figure. She had always been an attractive child, but as she became a teen, people could begin to see that Greta would grow into a great beauty.

Not only did Greta's body change when she reached her teenage years, but her intellectual development also saw changes. As was the custom with girls in Sweden, she ended her schooling at age 13, meaning she had received just 6 years of schooling. For the rest of her life, she would remain relatively uneducated, and after graduating, she lived with her grandparents, who remained in the countryside and never joined their children in the city.

In 1919, when Greta was 14, her father fell ill. At this time, the Spanish flu spread rapidly throughout the city, and Karl was just one of many locals who were gravely affected. This forced Sven and Anna to work while the younger Greta nursed her father (Payne). Nevertheless, he died a slow death and would pass away the following June, at just 48 years old.

After Karl's death, it was all the more imperative that Greta find employment. Her first job was as a soap-latherer in a barbershop, which lasted for a brief while, but she later got more desirable work in the PUB department store in Stockholm. The nature of her employment was fluid; sometimes she ran errands, but she also served in the millinery department (Swenson). Shortly thereafter, she was hired by PUB to model hats, a position that brought her greater exposure and eventually helped her become a fashion model. This early tenure at PUB reflects the oft-neglected influence of the department store - both in the United States and Europe - on furthering the acting careers of future film luminaries. Acclaimed director Vincente Minnelli, for example, worked as a shop window designer, and viewers can see vestiges of the shop window aesthetic in his design style as a director. The department store came complete with its own screen (the window), and its glamorous catalogue images made it a useful training ground for young actresses (Garbo) or directors and stage designers (Minnelli).

Obviously, Greta Garbo's life was filled with misfortune for the 15 years of her life, given her family's poverty and her father's death. But after that, her fortunes took a turn for the better. By late 1920, she was regularly appearing in film commercials for the department store, and after that went on for a couple of years, she was discovered by director Erik Arthur Petschler, who cast her in his short two-reel film *Peter the Tramp* (1922). This introduced Greta to the film industry, and while it would still be two years before her career picked up in earnest, she was, for all intents and purposes, an actress from this point forward.

Erik Arthur Petschler

Chapter 2: From Sweden to Germany to Hollywood

Peter the Tramp was a major event in Greta Garbo's life, but she still had a great deal of training to complete before she could be accepted as a viable star in the Swedish film industry, which was extremely competitive. While it's easily forgotten today, Sweden had an incredibly vibrant film industry during this period, and even though Hollywood had already staked its claim as the forerunner of the international cinematic landscape, national cinemas in Sweden, Germany, and elsewhere throughout Western Europe enjoyed great power during this period. Today, there is a misleading tendency to reduce all of Swedish cinema to the famous films of Ingmar Bergman, the much-lauded art-house director known for *The Seventh Seal* (1957), *Wild*

Strawberries (1957), and *Persona* (1968), but Bergman himself was heavily influenced by his forebears, and during the silent era Sweden was internationally recognized for the films of two other directors: Victor Sjostrom and Mauritz Stiller. The former, who would later star in *Wild Strawberries*, earned recognition for *Ingeborg Holm* (1913), one of the first masterpieces of Swedish cinema. His fame catapulted even further in 1920, when he directed *The Phantom Carriage*. Meanwhile, Stiller earned raves for *Sir Arne's Treasure* (1919). These films were immensely popular, not only in Sweden but worldwide. Growing up, Greta may have been more interested in theatre than cinema, but anyone growing up in Sweden could not ignore the opportunity for fame afforded by the motion picture industry there.

In 1922, after appearing in *Peter the Tramp*, Greta enrolled at The Royal Dramatic Theatre's Acting School in Stockholm. It's unclear how well she did at the Academy; in fact, it seems she was often late for her acting classes (Paris). That said, her tardiness should not be interpreted as arrogance but rather as shyness. Throughout her life, Garbo was extraordinarily shy, and as a young actress, she suffered from self-consciousness before the camera, which is ironic in light of the fact that she would later be renowned for looking so natural on-screen. Regardless of how well she did or didn't do, she continued to hone her craft, and there were few better places to do it than at the acclaimed Academy.

Greta's next major breakthrough came in 1923, when Mauritz Stiller elected to cast her in *The Saga of Gosta Berling* (1924). Since the film was made in Sweden, it is not as well-known as Garbo's Hollywood films, but the significance of the movie for her career cannot be overstated. After all, not only was she cast in a film directed by one of Sweden's great directors, she earned a starring role. Before she could star in the film, however, Stiller urged her to change her name, insisting that while Greta was acceptable, Gustafsson was too ubiquitous. "Garbo" was a far more distinctive name, and it paired well with her first name. This was actually not the first time Garbo changed her name, as she had eliminated an "s" from her surname in 1922, but that alone hadn't been sufficient for Stiller. After changing her last name altogether, Garbo was primed to star in a Mauritz Stiller film.

Greta in *The Saga of Gosta Berling*

Even though Garbo had spent much of the past two years studying acting at the Academy, her education essentially continued while acting in *The Saga of Gosta Berling*. Stiller operated as surrogate acting instructor, molding the star to suit his specifications, and in the process he became a mentor to her, a dynamic that would continue even after Garbo moved to Hollywood later in the decade. On its own merits, Garbo's first film with Stiller was quite successful, despite her inexperience; the success of the film was hardly surprising given the strength of the director and the fact that it was adapted from the acclaimed novel of the same name, which had been written by Nobel Prize-winning author Selma Lagerlof. In a role that establishes the regal connotations of her star persona, Garbo stars as Countess Elizabeth Dohna, who is in love with the eponymous Gosta Berling. Garbo's portrayal lacks the quiet confidence of her later performances, but her portrayal of the Countess was more in line with the novel from which the film was adapted. Regardless, Garbo's talent is on full display, particularly in the film's concluding scenes, which included a show-stopping sleigh ride through the Swedish landscape.

As was common with adaptations of the time period, Stiller did not care to condense the plot of the novel, and as a result Garbo is not actually present for much of the film. Due to its length (over three hours), the film is somewhat tedious for today's viewers, and in its entirety, the movie was released in two parts, although for its international release it was condensed to one installment (with the exception of Norway and Finland, which received the complete edition.) Antiquated as it might now appear, the movie was a major success, with Stiller and Garbo mutually benefitting from one another. For Garbo, Stiller brought her instant credibility, while Stiller was able to take credit for the still-relatively undiscovered actress. Their lives to this point could not have been more different - Stiller was 22 years older and significantly more famous - yet they formed a lucrative partnership that would later see them leave for Hollywood together.

Stiller

Building on the success *of The Saga of Gosta Berling*, Garbo was cast in *The Joyless Street* (1925), a high-profile German film directed by G.W. Pabst and co-starring Asta Nielson. The film marked a significant departure from most German films of the time; while the films of Fritz Lang, F.W. Murnau, and Robert Wiene were German Expressionist, Pabst's film was the first in the still-young New Objectivity movement. By 1925, his career was still young, and after being mesmerized by *The Saga of Gosta Berling*, he arranged for Garbo to star in his next film. He was fortunate that Garbo was even available; in late 1924, she and Stiller had arranged to make a film set in Turkey, but the financial backing fell through, leading Garbo to sign on to appear in Pabst's film.

Fortunately for Garbo, Pabst was every bit as talented as Stiller, and her reputation would not suffer from *The Joyless Street*. Unlike the stylization of Wiene's *The Cabinet of Dr. Caligari* (1921) or Lang's *Dr. Mabuse, The Gambler* (1924), *The Joyless Street* featured a realistic setting and plot that offers a powerful glimpse of the anxieties of post-World War I Vienna, with Garbo and Nielson starring as impoverished women who attempt to steer themselves toward upward mobility. Nielson's character becomes a prostitute, while Garbo's character resists prostitution and is rewarded when she meets and falls in love with a man working for the American Red Cross. To be certain, the film relies on its happy ending, but it also provided a degree of social realism that was largely unseen at the time and would be expanded upon by Pabst in later films such as *Pandora's Box* (1929) and *Diary of a Lost Girl* (1929).

Garbo in *The Joyless Street*

As strong a film as *The Joyless Street* was, Stiller had not been involved in it, and he would not be separated from his star actress for long. By the mid-1920s, both Stiller and Garbo were gaining strong reputations, not only within Western Europe but even in Hollywood, though the exact circumstances that brought Garbo to Hollywood are not entirely clear. According to Karen Swenson, the director and vice president of Metro-Goldwyn-Mayer, Louis B. Mayer, was interested in bringing Stiller to the United States. He sent Irving Thalberg, his head of production, to Sweden in order to hire Stiller, but Stiller was adamant in demanding that Garbo be included in the contract, so Thalberg hired them both (Swenson).

However, it has also been asserted that Thalberg and Mayer were always more interested in Garbo than Stiller (Viera), and considering how the studio subsequently treated Stiller, it seems more likely that this latter scenario is correct. According to Mayer's daughter, after he saw Garbo in *The Saga of Gosta Berling*, Mayer remarked, "It was her eyes. I can make a star out of her." She remembered that Mayer was desperate to get Garbo any way he could: "This director is wonderful but what we really ought to look at is the girl.... The girl, look at the girl!...I'll take her without him. I'll take her with him. Number one is the girl."

Mayer

In any event, it was clear that Stiller and Garbo were not interested in separating from one another, so they were brought over to America together in June 1925. Although they were coming at the behest of MGM, Garbo and Stiller did not head directly to Hollywood. Instead, they arrived in New York City and remained on the East Coast for a full three months while awaiting instruction from MGM. Frustrated by the lack of response, Stiller arranged for Garbo to take photographs with Arnold Genthe, a notable photographer, and eventually, the photographs found their way to Mayer. In the late summer, Garbo and Stiller traveled across the country, and Garbo signed her contract in late August, upon which she was to undergo the typical process of physical transformation that took place whenever actresses signed with a studio. In Garbo's case, there was a fairly substantial difference between her appearance upon arriving in Hollywood and the look she would later perfect in her storied Hollywood films. First of all, she was moderately heavier, and while actresses were typically heavier in the mid-1920s than they are in the 21st century, Mayer and Thalberg still arranged for Garbo to diet. Second, Garbo's hair was made softer, and she also received substantial periodontal work (Paris). All of this took place before she appeared in a film for MGM; her first film with the studio, *Torrent*, was not released until February 1926.

Chapter 3: Queen of the Late Silent Era

"Her face darkens with a slight tightening around the eyes and mouth; she registers a passing idea with a contraction of her brows or a drooping of her lids. Worlds turned on her movements" – David Denby, film critic.

Given the fact it took half a year before a film with Garbo in it was released, it's clear that Garbo initially received a cool reception from the studio, and Stiller was treated no better. In fact, director Monta Bell required a female lead for *Torrent* only because of the withdrawal of Norma Shearer. Garbo seized the opportunity at Stiller's urging, but the experience would prove onerous. Her co-star, Ricardo Cortez, disrespected her, and Bell treated her poorly as well (Paris). It is also painfully obvious that Garbo was not the first choice for the part; in the film, she plays a lowly showgirl, a role that clashed poorly with her shy disposition. The film is truly Cortez's picture, as he was one of the leading actors in Hollywood at the time, and it marked something of an unfortunate inauguration to Hollywood for Garbo. Still, her performance earned strong reviews, and the movie performed quite well at the box office despite mixed reviews.

Cortez and Garbo in *Torrent*

Pleased with the commercial success of *Torrent*, as well as the positive press for Garbo's performance, Thalberg wasted little time in arranging for Garbo's next picture, *The Temptress* (1926). Greta was pleased to learn Stiller was assigned to direct the film, but it proved to be a terrible match for both of them. As the title suggests, the film featured Garbo in a flapper-style role, not unlike her character from *Torrent*. Why MGM believed that Garbo was well-suited to playing flappers is not clear, since they were aware of her shyness and timidity before the camera; in fact, she was so shy that she started to prohibit people from visiting her on set, explaining, "If I am by myself, my face will do things I cannot do with it otherwise."

Furthermore, Stiller was poorly-suited for the film and clashed with the film's co-star, Antonio Moreno. Thalberg, who had grown tired of Stiller even before the film began, fired Stiller and replaced him with Fred Niblo, after which the scenes Stiller had completed were reshot, making *The Tempress* an incredibly expensive film. As with Garbo's first film, it received mixed reviews, even as Garbo was lauded for her performance and the film performed quite well as the box office. By this point, it was becoming clear that Garbo was a rising star in Hollywood, and Thalberg displayed his marketing savvy as the studio's production head by giving Garbo top billing. It may seem strange to watch Garbo as a Roaring Twenties flapper, but she dominated the screen nonetheless.

With the success of *Torrent* and *The Temptress*, Garbo had amply demonstrated that she did not need to be tethered to Mauritz Stiller, and as it turned out, she would never again work with the director who brought her to prominence in Sweden. Instead of pairing Garbo with the famed Swedish director, MGM arranged for a different sort of partnership by repeatedly casting Garbo alongside John Gilbert. The first of these films was *Flesh of the Devil* (1926), yet another movie that cast Garbo in a flapper-style role. She plays Felicitas, a married woman who becomes romantically involved with a pair of friends, but in the end, both men choose their friendship over their relationship with Garbo's character, who dies at the film's conclusion. The movie is shocking for its fairly overt sexuality, even by 21st century standards, and Garbo continued to prove that she could play the role of the female siren to great effect. In fact, her performance in this film was sexier than any of her more famous portrayals, mostly because the film could never have passed the more draconian censorship standards that were implemented in the following decade. From the early 1930s through the end of Garbo's career, the Hays Code would prevent any frank displays of sexuality, and much of the novelty of viewing *Flesh of the Devil* or Garbo's earlier Hollywood films is seeing Garbo in a role so entirely dissimilar from her storied performances in films such as *Queen Christina* or *Ninotchka*.

Garbo and Gilbert in *Flesh and the Devil*

In the end, *Flesh of the Devil* proved to be the last of Garbo's flapper performances, but she offered a similarly erotic portrayal in her next film, *Love* (1927). An adaptation of Tolstoy's *Anna Karenina*, the movie casts Garbo in the headlining role of Anna Karenina, with Gilbert playing Alexei Vronsky. Again, Greta and her co-star displayed great chemistry, helping cement their reputation as arguably the premier on-screen romantic couple of the second half of the 1920s. One revealing bit of movie trivia is that *Love* contained two separate endings, one for its domestic audience and another released in Europe. In the American ending, Anna, her child, and Vronsky are united, an ending typical of classical Hollywood, but in the more tragic European ending, Garbo's character commits suicide, an ending more faithful to Tolstoy's novel. The film is fascinating in part because it was forced to veer away from either the novel or the conventions of the film industry, and the American ending is a testament to the sheer potency of the Hollywood system, which overrode even a famous source text like *Anna Karenina*.

The American ending of *Love* was certainly unsettling for viewers expecting a faithful rendition of Tolstoy's famous text, but at the same time, the fact that there was a separate ending for European viewers reflects the magnitude of Garbo's star power, even at this time. Garbo was even more beloved in her native land, and European audiences were willing to embrace a film in which she died at the conclusion, a reflection of tragedy being a convention of German and Swedish cinema during the silent era. As popular as Garbo was in the United States, she was a national icon in Sweden and throughout Western Europe, and MGM was forever tasked with ensuring that her films were palatable to her foreign followers. Indeed, the foreign audience was perhaps the greatest trump card Garbo held over her competitors in Hollywood; even if American viewers did not particularly care for a film of hers, she could rely on a worshipful Swedish audience. Garbo was one of the earliest examples of the sheer internationalization of cinema as an art form.

After *Love*, Garbo was afforded the opportunity to star in a film directed by Victor Sjostrom, who by this time was already working in Hollywood. Unfortunately, the movie, *The Divine Woman* (1928), is almost entirely lost, a great shame in light of Sjostrom's formidable talents. In the film, which is set in 19th century France, Garbo plays a girl who has grown up in the French countryside but moves to Paris, where she rises to prominence as an actress. Although the fact that the film is lost makes it difficult to analyze it in any close detail, one can see how the film portrays the dual dimensions of the Garbo persona, coupling the "naturalness" of the rural girl from the countryside with the ability to be a mesmerizing actress. *The Divine Woman* was a moderate success, but Garbo would never again work with Sjostrom.

Building on the success of *Love*, Garbo and Gilbert were paired together on several additional occasions throughout the rest of the decade. In 1928, they starred in *A Woman of Affairs*, which would prove to be her greatest triumph to this point in her career. The incredibly melodramatic plot charts the lives of three childhood friends, all wealthy members of the British aristocracy. Two of the friends, Diana (Garbo) and David, marry, but David secretly operates as a thief and kills himself out of the knowledge that he will inevitably be brought to justice by the police. After her husband's death, Diana marries the other third friend, Neville (played by Gilbert). As with *Love*, Garbo and Gilbert display a natural chemistry that was adored by domestic and international audiences alike. It is also worth noting the presence of Lewis Stone, a relatively minor actor but one who would be a recurring presence in Garbo's films, appearing in seven Garbo films in total.

A Woman of Affairs grossed more than a $1.3 million at the box office and made Garbo the highest-grossing star at the studio. Perhaps more importantly, it finally demonstrated to the American viewing public that Garbo was capable of excelling in roles that were more complex and dramatic than the flapper portrayals she had given earlier in the decade. As *New York Telegraph* reviewer Pierre de Rohan put it, "She has a glamour and fascination for both sexes which have never been equaled on the screen."

Garbo in *A Woman of Affairs*

Perhaps not surprisingly given all the time they spent together, the partnership between Garbo and Gilbert extended beyond their professional capacities. The two lived together for a time and were assumed to be romantically involved during the late 1920s (Swenson). That Greta and her famous co-star were great friends cannot be disputed, but the question of whether the two were actually romantically involved remains unanswered. It is well-known that Gilbert was at least bisexual if not gay, and Garbo's sexuality was always well-guarded, but it is similarly believed that she was gay. She never married or had children, and as she grew older, she maintained several relatively high-profile romantic relations with women. However, in 1920s America, it was impossible for an actor to thrive by being publicly homosexual, and the relationship between Gilbert and Garbo may have been platonic and a simple arrangement of convenience. Regardless of the motives behind it, the off-screen pairing could not have been more ideal for MGM, which could advertise the romantic relationship – both on and off the screen – of two of its most significant stars.

By now, it was clear that Garbo was the ideal actress for MGM, as she embodied the image of the pure woman that they would perfect even further over the course of the next decade. As Jane Ellen Wayne notes, the actresses at MGM were expected to maintain strict standards of decorum and decentness, a standard that Garbo played to the hilt: "Married or not, the MGM girls maintained their virginal image. They were above sex, an untouchable breed of womanhood. We pictured them in the bridal bed with every coiffed hair in place and their make-up impeccable" (xi). As this description makes clear, the fact that Garbo was not married didn't mar her public image but enhanced it, making her seem more virginal. This image of Garbo as the pure, untouched beauty was certainly far removed from her early flapper portrayals, but it also contributed to her reputation for being icy, something that would be far more enduring.

Surprisingly, *A Woman of Affairs* would actually be the final film of the decade starring Garbo and Gilbert together. Greta's next movie was *Wild Orchids* (1929), which paired her with Lewis Stone. The melodrama features Garbo as Lillie, a housewife whose husband, John (Stone), pays little attention to her. Thanks to her exotic beauty, Lillie quickly gets the attention of other men, but she and her husband reconcile at the film's conclusion. Despite receiving lukewarm reviews, the movie was an incredible commercial success, again grossing more than $1 million. It offered implicit proof that in the Garbo-Gilbert films, it was Greta who was the main attraction, and she could succeed regardless of her co-star.

Wild Orchids was only the first of four films Garbo would star in during that year, making 1929 the busiest year of her career. Her other films from 1929 include *A Man's Man*, *The Single Standard*, and *The Kiss*. Of these, the latter two are the most interesting, for different reasons. In *The Single Standard*, Garbo plays Arden, a woman who craves freedom in her romantic quests, and after a couple of romances, she marries longtime friend Tommy (played by Johnny Mack Brown). They have a child together, but Arden still yearns for her independence. However, at the film's conclusion, she comes to value her family and redirects her attention toward raising her child. The plot is of course yet another Garbo melodrama from the decade, yet it is particularly worthy of interest for its depiction of gender. Indeed, the film hints at an expression of female desire that need not result in a life of quiet domesticity; even if the Hollywood ending suppresses this, Garbo still provides a convincing image of strong femininity.

Garbo in *Wild Orchids*

Meanwhile, *The Kiss* remains fascinating for the way in which it reveals the pressures that that the film industry faced during the late 1920s, especially MGM. The movie, another Garbo melodrama, was the final silent film made by the studio; by 1929, synchronized sound was a relatively new phenomenon, but it had been used in films such as *The Jazz Singer* (1927) and *Sunrise* (1927), the former released by Warner Brothers and the latter by Fox. By the end of the decade, it had been clear for several years that sound cinema would soon be a reality, the result of a convergence of sorts between cinema and radio. However, MGM had been especially resistant to implement sound, and it is not difficult to see why. The studio was not actually behind the time - it had been the first to implement Technicolor - and it is worth noting that they had in fact made a sound film in 1928 (*The Viking*), albeit one with no dialogue. It would not be until two years later that they would produce their first "talkie".

One of the problems MGM faced was making a sound film with Greta Garbo, due to the fear that her foreign accent might alienate American audiences. As conveyed to comic effect in *Singin' in the Rain* (1953), all of the major silent cinema icons were crucially threatened by sound, with Charlie Chaplin perhaps the most representative example. In silent films, viewers from around the world could superimpose their own accents onto the character, but with the advent of sound, someone like Chaplin was finally marked by his voice. In a similar vein,

Garbo's accent would finally mark her as clearly Swedish, and while Swedes did not suffer any great discrimination, there was still risk that Garbo would lose her universal appeal as a result. At the same time, the preeminent silent film star, Charlie Chaplin, would not voice any dialogue until *Modern Times*, which was not released until 1936, and that hurt his popularity as "talkies" became the standard. MGM avoided casting Garbo in a talkie for a long time, but they inevitably realized there was no way for their top actress to forever remain a silent actress. As a result, the new decade would need a new Garbo.

Chapter 4: Garbo Talks!

As it turned out, the introduction of synchronized sound proved fortuitous for Garbo, who had one of the most successful years of her career in 1930. Her first film that year was *Anna Christie*, which remains famous simply for being the first picture in which Garbo's voice could be heard. The studio marketed the film heavily by adopting the now famous phrase "Garbo talks!" The movie was an adaptation of the play of the same title by Eugene O'Neill, and Greta plays the 20-year old daughter of the head of a coal barge. Long estranged from her father, she writes him to tell him that she will live with him; as unglamorous as her father's work is, hers is equally so, as she serves as a prostitute prior to relocating. While staying with her father, she meets a sailor and overcomes her anxiety and shame over her rough past.

As this plot outline suggests, *Anna Christie* not only broke from Garbo's films on a formal level (through the introduction of sound) but also in the narrative. While she had played flappers in her first Hollywood movies, Garbo's films from the past couple of years had been glamorous, elegant melodramas, a far cry from the gritty realism of *Anna Christie*. The roughness of her character is reflected in her first line of dialogue, in which she orders a drink: "Gimme a whiskey, ginger ale on the side, and don't be stingy, baby." But far from being alienated by hearing Garbo speak, audiences appreciated her all the more, and the movie was the highest-grossing film of 1930. To be sure, a large measure of the film's success can simply be attributed to the novelty inherent in getting to watch Greta Garbo speak before the camera, but to chalk up the film's success solely to its use of sound disregards its cultural context. For an American public caught in the throes of the Great Depression, viewing a downtrodden Greta Garbo was also alluring because it made her all the more accessible to domestic viewers. At the same time, Greta's precious European audience would not have appreciated seeing her speaking English, so versions were made in several other languages as well. For today's viewers, *Anna Christie* may lack the drama of Garbo's films from later in the decade, but it was a tremendous success on all fronts. Greta was nominated for an Academy Award for Best Actress (although this nomination was also for her performance in *Romance*, released later in the same year), while director Clarence Brown was also nominated.

Garbo in *Anna Christie*

The success of *Anna Christie* reflects the way in which European directors and stars enjoyed great popularity in America during the late 1920s and 1930s, a trend best exhibited by Garbo and her great rival, Marlene Dietrich. 1930 also proved to be a significant year for Dietrich, who rose to prominence on the success of *The Blue Angel*, which has aged even better than *Anna Christie*. The similarities between Greta and Dietrich are plenty, and comparing them illuminates a lot about both women's careers. Even though Garbo was from Sweden and Dietrich from Germany, they each rose to fame in their native land before relocating to the United States, and as Alex Doty notes, Garbo and Dietrich were also linked to prominent expatriate directors: Garbo with Stiller and Dietrich with Josef von Sternberg. While it is true that von Sternberg was far more successful in Hollywood than Stiller had been, the two directors both initially exerted a svengali-like degree of control over their actresses (Doty). Each stunning in their European beauty, Garbo and Dietrich captivated American viewers with their exotic sexuality and their icy comportment before the camera.

Dietrich

While many similarities exist between the two great European émigrés, Greta was also different from Dietrich in important ways. First, Garbo was better-loved in her native land, and she was able to rely upon a European base that Dietrich simply lacked. This would allow Garbo to remain immensely profitable even after her stock began to slip in Hollywood later in the decade. Moreover, even though Garbo could certainly play a showgirl, she lacked the natural singing talents of Dietrich, and it is no accident that Dietrich became famous through films that saw her play stage performers, such as *The Blue Angel*, *Morocco* (1930) and *Blonde Venus* (1932). Perhaps most notably, Garbo was never as overtly sexual as Dietrich, who challenged American standards of sexual decorum on-screen. The differences between the two stars were immediately recognized by the entertainment industry, and Paramount (the studio that signed Dietrich) urged the media to create a rivalry between the two actresses. As a result, Dietrich was the greatest competitor Garbo faced during her career.

The rivalry between the two actresses also extended beyond the confines of their professional lives. Notorious for her bisexuality, Dietrich had an affair with Mercedes de Acosta, who, as Ruiz and Korrol notes, was something of a renegade figure in Hollywood: "An important figure in the café society…Acosta influenced a generation of public figures who challenged sexual politics, refused conformity with sexual norms, and saw themselves as their own unique invention" (189). Garbo first met de Acosta through her friend Salka Viertel, who herself was romantically linked with Garbo, and together, Garbo and de Acosta formed what Rodger Streitmatter has termed an "outlaw marriage," consisting of "unions that defied the laws and mores of their day" (Wallace). Obviously, Garbo was never married in a legal sense, but her relationship with de Acosta was unusual for the era.

Mercedes de Acosta

Even though Dietrich was married at the time, throughout her career she maintained numerous affairs with both men and women, and one of those women was de Acosta, even as she was with Garbo. The American public may not have been aware of the lesbian rivalry between Garbo and Dietrich that centered on de Acosta, but the romantic exploits were well-known within the industry. Despite de Acosta's unfaithfulness, she and Garbo remained together for the rest of Garbo's career, finally breaking apart in 1943 (Schanke).

After *Anna Christie*, Garbo's career stagnated for a brief while, but she did earn acclaim for her performance in *Romance*, and early in 1931, she appeared in *Inspiration* and *Susan Lenox (Her Fall and Rise)*. While both movies were unsuccessful, her career rebounded later in the year when she was cast in *Mata Hari* (1931). Starring in the title role, Garbo plays an exotic dancer who secretly works as a German spy, and the film contains a surprisingly grim ending. However, it is perhaps best remembered for the incredibly stylized dance sequences, which rival the famous dances Marlene Dietrich performed in her films with von Sternberg. The film forms a clear counterpoint with *Anna Christie*, returning Greta to the seductress roles she performed immediately after arriving in Hollywood. Audiences across the world loved the film, and even though it was not nominated for any Academy Awards, it stands as one of her most adored films. Film critics note that *Mata Hari* may have represented the pinnacle of Garbo's popularity, and it was noted that the release of the film "caused a panic"; in New York, " police reserves [were] required to keep the waiting mob in order."

Garbo in *Inspiration*

Mata Hari was crucial in bringing Garbo back after the three unsuccessful films she appeared in following *Anna Christie*, and the movie set into motion a string of great successes. Garbo's next film, *Grand Hotel*, was her only one to earn an Oscar for Best Picture, although truthfully speaking, whether it deserved this honor is open for debate. The film muscled its way to its Academy Award victory through an all-star cast that included not only Garbo but also John Barrymore, Lionel Barrymore, and Joan Crawford. *Grand Hotel* also boasted tremendous production values, as Irving Thalberg arranged for the acclaimed Cedric Gibbons to head the artistic design. The complex storyline features Garbo as Gruninskaya, a Russian ballerina who becomes romantically involved with the Baron (Barrymore), but he is killed at the end of the film. At one point, Garbo states "I want to be alone," a line that would come to define her public image. The melodramatic plot, which sees none of the characters happy at the film's conclusion, did not privilege any of its leading characters over one another; for example, Garbo and Crawford occupy roughly equal ground. This equal standing perhaps contributed to the remarkable fact that none of the characters were even nominated for an Academy Award, the only time in history that the Best Picture-winning film failed to have a star nominated.

Garbo and Barrymore in *Grand Hotel*

With the success of Grand Hotel, Greta Garbo was not only the premier star at MGM but also in Hollywood. By this time, "Garbomania" was in full effect, and as a result, Garbo was earning between $250,000-300,000 per film (Swenson). No actress in history had ever commanded such profits. How did Garbo manage to accomplish this? Garbo's appeal is nicely articulated by film theorist Rudolf Arnheim, who gets at the heart of the effect Garbo had on male viewers: "Above her smile are the arched eyebrows like two circumflexes, meant to show that this smile is always imbued with quiet, sarcastic suffering. It is only when she looks at a man's mouth that this woman suddenly becomes deadly serious, as though she were enjoying the sight of the sacraments…On quiet cat's feet, her coat pulled tightly about her and her hands folded in her lap, Greta Garbo passes censorship. And every evening in the theater, three hundred men are unfaithful to their wives." (216-17).

This description addresses how Garbo was sensual but delicate, connecting with the viewer on a visceral level but not over-the-top in her expression of female sexuality. However, as a result of her great fame, Greta began exercising her authority more assertively and made extensive demands, which included banning media and studio officials from her film sets. In 1932, Garbo also signed a more lucrative contract with MGM that gave her heightened control over her films, a privilege that was routinely denied at the time because film studios effectively treated their actors as indentured servants. The fact Garbo was able to negotiate such an arrangement attests to the way in which she could not be contained by the industry.

Garbo's films often starred the same leading men, and in 1932, a new partnership was born, this time with Melvyn Douglas. Garbo and Douglas first appeared together in *As You Desire Me*, which also had famed director Erich von Stroheim. The convoluted plot involves Garbo as a nightclub performer, and in a sense, the film combines the harsh realism of *Anna Christie* with the show business theatrics of *Grand Hotel*. Garbo's character is an alcoholic, and the narrative centers on her lack of memory, as it is revealed that she may in fact be an Italian Countess. Unfortunately, *As You Desire Me* was marred by conflicts during its production, with von Stroheim constantly at odds with Irving Thalberg. Garbo, a strong supporter of von Stroheim, exercised her authority in order to keep her friend on board, but the film was not particularly successful and is arguably more interesting for the production circumstances than for its confusing narrative.

Given her reputation for being reclusive, people have often questioned whether Garbo actually enjoyed acting. Throughout her life, Garbo maintained many friendships and traveled on a frequent basis, but at the same time, Garbo never appeared to embrace acting as a profession, despite the fact that it literally raised her from the lowest dredges of poverty to a life of great privilege. That said, some thought Garbo's acting offered her an escape from her own life; as actress Marie Dressler asserted, "Garbo is lonely. She always has been and she always will be. She lives in the core of a vast aching aloneness. She is a great artist, but it is both her supreme glory and her supreme tragedy that art is to her the only reality. The figures of living men and women, the events of everyday existence, move about her, shadowy, unsubstantial. It is only when she breathes the breath of life into a part, clothes with her own flesh and blood the concept of a playwright, that she herself is fully awake, fully alive."

Greta's ambivalence toward her career was apparent in 1932, because after the conclusion of *As You Desire Me*, Garbo announced that she would quit acting. She even went so far as to board a ship headed for Europe once filming was completed, but she was ultimately convinced to return and would remain an actress for the remainder of the decade. While Garbo stuck around for several more years, it's clear that she was less enthralled with her craft than several of her contemporaries; unlike Bette Davis or Katharine Hepburn, she would not remain an actress well into her old age.

The saga of Garbo's contemplated retirement took her away from acting for about 18 months, but her comeback film, *Queen Christina* (1933), was worth the wait and arguably her most famous performance. A historical drama, Garbo plays the eponymous Queen Christina of Sweden, and she used her clout at MGM to ensure that John Gilbert would serve as her co-star and play the role of the Spaniard, Antonio. By this time, Gilbert was far from MGM's top choice and had fallen from leading man status. Like Chaplin, the introduction of sound had crippled his career, as audiences could not embrace his voice. Looking past his voice, however, the chemistry between Gilbert and Garbo is a highlight of the film and reflects Garbo's savvy.

Garbo in *Queen Christina*

Like most Hollywood historical dramas, the film is very liberal in its portrayal of historical events, with the most dramatic alteration being the love affair between Queen Christina and Antonio, a fictionalized romance that did not actually take place. Considering that *Queen Christina* was a Hollywood film, there was simply no possibility that MGM would fund a big-budget film that did not centrally involve a romance, and this was especially the case given that it was Garbo's comeback picture. Still, several of the movie's more famous scenes, particularly the depiction of the Thirty Years' War, are accurate and memorable. Not only was Garbo a natural fit to portray a royal figure, but it is worth noting that the film indirectly furthered the rivalry between Garbo and Marlene Dietrich, who one year later played the role of Catherine the Great in *The Scarlett Empress* (1934).

Of the two films, it is *Queen Christina* that has stood the test of time better, likely because there is perhaps no role that better encapsulates the image of Greta Garbo than her portrayal of the famous Swedish queen. Indeed, the defiant loneliness of her portrayal reflects a perfect harmony between Greta Garbo and her character in the film. Richard Dyer mentioned how this dynamic may have worked on viewers of the movie: "It would be a sign of mental disorder to believe that Greta Garbo actually was Queen Christina. What I think is the case, however, is that the roles and/or the performance of a star in a film were taken as revealing the personality of the star (which then was corroborated by the stories in the magazines, etc." (22). While the same could perhaps be said for any movie character, what was especially unusual in the case of Queen Christina is the perfect synthesis achieved between Garbo and her character. No other actress could portray the deft balance between sensuality and guardedness that Garbo did, and there is no denying that she dominates the film with her performance.

In fact, *Queen Christina* is responsible for providing perhaps the most iconic image of Garbo's career: the shot of her at the film's conclusion, perched defiantly at the bow of her ship, headed for Spain. As the final shot of the movie, it is at once beautiful and enigmatic, doubling as the signature shot of her career. For the shot, director Rouben Mamoulian famously instructed for Garbo to do nothing at all, and her image is composed but also the very picture of naturalness (Dyer). This natural quality also manifests through the fact that, as Mamoulian notes, Garbo always disliked rehearsing. Early in her career, she could not have gotten away with this, but in later films such as *Queen Christina*, viewers can get the sense that her performances are pure and unrehearsed (Stevens, Jr.).

Queen Christina was a major hit at the box office, grossing more than double its expensive $1.1 million budget, but surprisingly, Garbo was not nominated for any Academy Awards as a result of the film. Of course, audiences still eagerly anticipated her work, including the ultimately unremarkable *The Painted Veil* (1934), While critics didn't care much for that film, reviewer Andre Sennwald wrote in *The New York Times*, "She is the most miraculous blend of personality and sheer dramatic talent that the screen has ever known and her presence in *The Painted Veil* immediately makes it one of the season's cinema events."

Garbo returned with a tour de force performance in *Anna Karenina* (1935). She had already played the heroine in a filmic adaptation of that Tolstoy novel earlier in her career (*Love*), but the 1935 version is significantly better-known and grossed more than $2 million. With the benefit of years of experience, her performance is more self-assured and defiant in the latter iteration. She plays a very strong-willed Anna Karenina, one whose tragic fate belies her ability to withstand tremendous adversity. Greta also benefitted from a strong supporting cast that included Basil Rathbone, Fredric March, and Maureen O'Sullivan. She was not nominated for an Oscar, but her performance did earn her the New York Film Critics Circle Award for Best Actress.

Garbo followed the success of *Anna Karenina* with *Camille* (1936), which earned her an Academy Award nomination for Best Actress and remains one of the more romantic films ever made. As with so many of her movies, Greta is cast in the title role and plays a woman who rises from poverty to reach the upper crust of Parisian society, but ultimately, she is unable to dissociate herself from her past and sacrifices her romance out of the knowledge that her sordid upbringing would tarnish the reputation of her wealthy lover. Yet again, Garbo's character dies at the conclusion of the film, this time of tuberculosis. The fact that Garbo dies at the end of several of her films constitutes one way in which she broke from the conventions of Hollywood cinema, but in a sense, the tragic endings supported her image as a steadfast, independent woman who resists male intervention and is all the more heroic for it. Her character may die at the conclusion of *Camille*, but it is impossible to view the picture without getting the sense that Garbo is a particularly strong female at a time in which women were commonly represented as damsels-in-distress.

Before 1937, it appeared as though Greta Garbo could do no wrong. She did not always give the impression that she enjoyed her craft, but there was no doubting her ability to turn massive profits. This would change, however, with *Conquest*, her lone film from 1937. Another historical drama, she plays the Countess Marie Walewska, who agrees to romance Napoleon Bonaparte out of the belief that it will save her native Poland. However, when Bonaparte marries the Archduchess Marie Louise of Austria, Garbo's character leaves Napoleon. The movie offers another representation of Garbo as the strong, regal female, and the strength of Garbo's performance and its superb production values made it entertaining in its own right. However, the production values, not to mention Garbo's salary, drove up the cost of the film. Despite grossing more than $2 million, Conquest lost more than $1 million.

The poor box office performance of *Conquest* highlights one of the dilemmas inherent in the film industry. As a result of the exorbitant salaries they commanded, the more famous a star became, the more difficult it was to recoup the costs and turn a profit in the films starring them. Furthermore, by the late 1930s, Garbo no longer had quite the clout she had enjoyed earlier in the decade. In 1938, she was one of several actresses, along with Marlene Dietrich, Norma Shearer, Joan Crawford, and Katharine Hepburn, famously labeled "Box Office Poison" by the National Theater Distributors of America (Chandler). This designation in no way signaled the end of her career, and the other actresses featured also managed to rebound, but it was evidence that Greta's films could no longer count on a healthy box office return.

After *Conquest*, MGM realized that a change was needed for Garbo, and in 1939 she starred in *Ninotchka*, her first comedy. Directed by the great comedic director Ernst Lubitsch, Garbo plays the title role, portraying a woman who becomes romantically involved with three jewel thieves she initially intends to bring to justice. The movie is as famous for its marketing campaign as the film itself; taking full advantage of the fact that Garbo had never before appeared in a comedy, MGM advertised the film with the phrase "Garbo Laughs!". This, of course, intentionally paralleled their earlier marketing of *Anna Christie*, which had been advertised with the phrase "Garbo Talks!"

Naturally, the opportunity to view Garbo in a new light proved irresistible to movie viewers, and *Ninotchka* became one of the most successful films of her career. At the same time, it would be a mistake to attribute the film's triumph to the novelty of watching Greta laugh, since she had laughed on-screen even in her most dramatic roles. The major difference was simply that this film was a comedy. In any event, after the disastrous *Conquest*, *Ninotchka* proved ideal as a sophisticated comedy that was not only entertaining but received excellent reviews. It was nominated for four Academy Awards, including one for Garbo's performance, and it rivals *Queen Christina* among the very best movies of her career.

Garbo with Melvyn Douglas in *Ninotchka*

Chapter 5: Retirement

"Except physically, we know little more about Garbo than we know about Shakespeare." – Kenneth Tynan

"The mystery surrounding Garbo was as thick as a London fog." - Tallulah Bankhead

After *Ninotchka*, MGM faced a dilemma, as they had to determine whether to continue casting Garbo in comedies or returning her to historical dramas. They opted for the former, casting her in George Cukor's *Two-Faced Woman* (1941), in which she plays two roles, one as Karin Borg and the other as her twin, Katherine Borg. However, her performance in the romantic comedy is shockingly over-the-top compared to her earlier films, and critics responded negatively. The movie actually performed moderately well in America, but the reviews of Garbo's performance were humiliating.

As it turned out, *Two-Faced Woman* signaled the end of Garbo's career, even if no one recognized it at the time. That said, the demise of her career cannot merely be reduced to the failure of her last picture, especially since it performed better than some of her other films. Rather, Garbo's career was threatened by the economic changes initiated by World War II. She had long relied upon her foreign demographic, but when the movie-going public in Europe diminished, her value deteriorated quickly (Paris). In 1942, she agreed to star in *The Girl from Leningrad* (1942), but the film fell through, and over the course of the decade, she would agree to several more projects, but none materialized (Viera). In 1948, she was offered a starring role in an adaptation of Balzac's *La Duchesse de Langlais*, but the film was aborted. The following year, she was offered the role of Norma Desmond in *Sunset Boulevard* (1950), but she turned it down. It might be fun to speculate how some of these films would have fared, but ultimately, *Two-Faced Woman* proved to be her final movie, meaning Garbo's film career was over when she was just 36 years old.

Despite retiring early, Garbo was never in need of money, and even though she had received scant formal education, she proved to be quite savvy with her own investments and never lacked funds. After retiring, she lived a relatively quiet life. In 1951, she became a citizen of the United States, and two years later, she purchased an apartment in Manhattan that she would live in for the rest of her life. She amused herself by traveling periodically, and also maintained an extensive art collection. Garbo maintained few friendships, but she was close to her maid, Claire Koger (Paris). She regularly took walks throughout New York City and remained healthy well into her 70s, despite admitting to bouts of depression (Swenson). Her health did not truly worsen until she was nearly 80 years old. In 1984, Garbo was successfully treated for breast cancer, and she did not die until six years later, passing away at age 84 due to pneumonia and renal failure (Paris).

Garbo signing her citizenship papers

There is no denying that Greta Garbo left an indelible imprint on film history, yet at the same time, there is an ahistorical quality to her. Indeed, she is one of the few actresses actually worthy of the distinction of being an icon, and she brought a mythical beauty with her even to those films that woefully miscast her as a flapper (as seen in her earliest Hollywood movies) or a comedienne (her final film). That Garbo was in so many mediocre films and never won an Academy Award seems entirely beside the point, because she personally transcended her movies. Garbo acted in some fine films, particularly during the 1930s, but no matter how inane or clever her plots may have been, watching Garbo remains the primary attraction when viewing her films. It is also the case that her legacy also extends beyond her physical appearance. She may not have been as radical in her sexuality as Marlene Dietrich, or as radical in defying social mores as Katharine Hepburn, but she was radical in her tranquility, effecting a headstrong femininity that broke away from the weak images of women that populated the cinema during her era.

While it is true that Garbo transcended her time, it is also important to place Garbo's accomplishments within the context of her time period. Her success was due in part to her deft ability to navigate from Sweden to Germany to Hollywood, as well as from silent films to talkies. While the premature end to her career might give the impression that she was unable to adapt, few actresses in film history were able to navigate such drastic changes within the industry as well as Garbo did. Moreover, her early retirement should not be interpreted as an act of resignation but rather a decision to leave a profession she no longer liked. In the end, more than half of her life was spent in retirement, and the simple rhythms of her retired life were a better match for her personality than the hectic schedule of a screen actress. If anything, the career of Greta Garbo should be analyzed for what it was, rather than what it might have been; she came and left quickly, but she conquered Hollywood during its Golden Age and will forever be recognized as one of film history's iciest queens.

A monument to Greta on the street where she was born, in Södermalm

Bibliography

Arnheim, Rudolf. Film Essays and Criticism. Madison: University of Wisconsin, 1997. Print.

Barthes, Roland. "The Face of Garbo." Mythologies. New York: Hill and Wang, 2001. 56-57. Print.

Chandler, Charlotte. I Know Where I'm Going: Katharine Hepburn, A Personal Biography. New York: Simon & Schuster, 2010. Print.

Doty, Alexander. "Marlene Dietrich and Greta Garbo: The Sexy Hausfrau versus the Swedish Sphinx." Glamour in a Golden Age: Movie Stars of the 1930s. Ed. Adreienne L. McLean. Piscataway: Rutgers, 2011. 108-128. Print.

Dyer, Richard. Stars. London: British Film Institute, 1979. Print.

Paris, Barry. Garbo. Minneapolis: University of Minnesota Press, 2002. Print.

Payne, Robert. The Great Garbo. New York: Cooper Square Press, 2002.

Ruiz, Vicki L., and Virginia Sanchez Korrol, eds. Latinas in the United States: A Historical Encyclopedia. Bloomington: Indiana University, 2006. Print.

Schanke, Robert A. That Furious Lesbian: The Story of Mercedes de Acosta. Carbondale: Southern Illinois University Press, 2004. Print.

Stevens, Jr., George. Conversations with the Great Moviemakers of Hollywood's Golden Age: At the American Film Institute. New York: Alfred A. Knopf, 2006. Print.

Streitmatter, Rodger. Outlaw Marriages: The Hidden Histories of Fifteen Extraordinary Same-Sex Couples. Boston: Beacon Press, 2012. Digital.

Swenson, Karen. Greta Garbo: A Life Apart. New York: Scribner, 1997. Print.

Viera, Mark A. Greta Garbo: A Cinematic Legacy. New York: Abrams, 2005. Print.

Wallace, David. Exiles in Hollywood. Pompton Plains: Limelight, 2006. Print.

Wayne, Jane Ellen. The Golden Girls of MGM: Greta Garbo, Joan Crawford, Lana Turner, Judy Garland, Ava Gardner, Grace Kelly, and Others. New York: Carroll and Graf, 2002. Print.

Made in the USA
Middletown, DE
10 March 2015